How to make your Paper Dinosaur:

1. Decide which style to build.
For each Paper Dinosaur, you have two pages... One with outlines for you to color yourself, and one is finished so you can just cut and fold. You can also use the outlines as a template to cut your Paper Dinosaur out of construction paper. This is a bit more advanced, but fun!

2. Setup your work area.
Always think about safety and easy access to your supplies when setting up your work area. Make sure to cover any furniture you are cutting or gluing on, which both protects and makes cleaning up easier!

3. Color, Cut, Fold and Glue.
Plan ahead and take your time, and be sure to go slowly around the curves. Some are tricky! Fold gently at first, and then pinch to make the fold tighter. Work out how you wish to glue a spot prior to gluing, and have patience to let it dry before handling further. For more hints & tips, check out the next page.

Mom or Dad want to help, too...
So just ask them :-)

www.paperdinosaurs.com
facebook.com/paperdinosaurs

Organize your work area for safety and easy acces to your tools

Curves can be tricky. Remember, it desn't have to be perfect

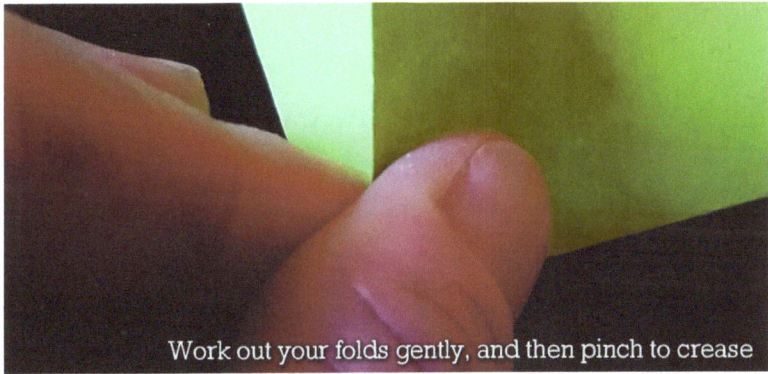
Work out your folds gently, and then pinch to crease

Try to use the least amount of glue, and wipe off any excess

PAPER DINOSAURS™ CUT AND FOLD COLORING BOOK. Written by Mark Butler. First printing. Published by Paper Dinosaurs Construction Co., CA 92602. Copyright and TM 2018 Paper Dinosaurs Construction Co. All rights reserved. All names and references in this publication are entirely fictional. No portion of this book may be reproduced by any means without express written consent by Paper Dinosaurs Construction Co. For information regarding press, media rights, foreign rights, licensing and anything else, please write us: info@paperdinosaurs.com

Paper Dinosaurs created by Mark Butler and Justin Hartfield. Illustrated by Diana Beltran Herrera and Mark Butler.

Paper Dinosaur Hints & Tips:

Adding the details.
Some Paper Dinosaurs have stripes, some have spots, and some have both! You can add these details when you are coloring, or cut them out of construction paper and glue them on. It's up to you!

Fold over before cutting, and get 2 for 1

Use other tools and paper types.
You will find that having clothing pins or small folder binders will help hold your pieces together while drying. A paper hole punch can really help making spots or a lot of berries fast and easy. And don't forget all the different types of paper there are... Sandpaper is great for beaches, and cardboard can be used to provide support!

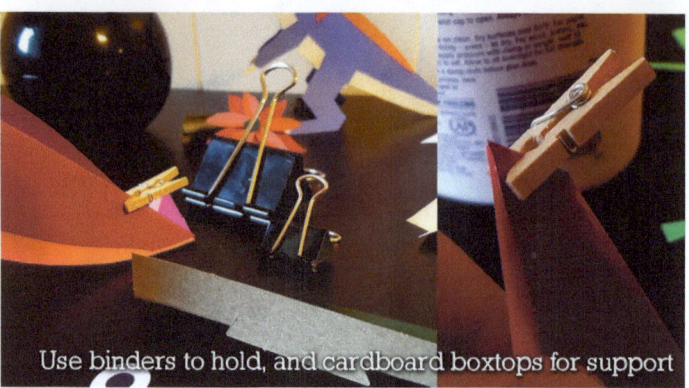
Use binders to hold, and cardboard boxtops for support

Build a diorama.
Paper Dinosaurs live in a huge world made of plants, flowers, fruits and veggies. Creating these, and posing your Paper Dinosaurs in them, is a great way to display your hard work. With so many varieties of plants and landscapes, it can take a lot of extra work to make your diorama look dense. So, it's best to start simple, and build from there. Layout your landscape first, and then add easy to cut and fold elements, like grass, in layers, using different colors of construction paper!

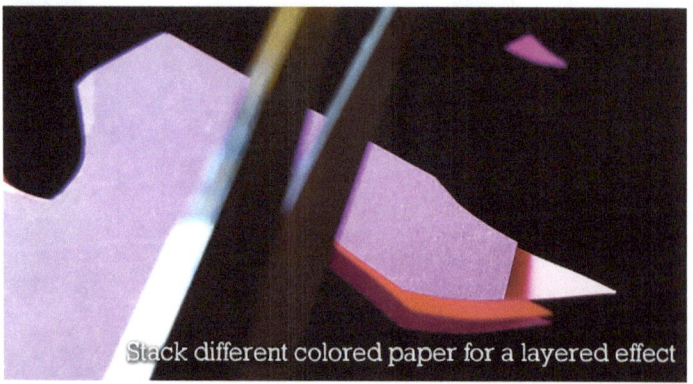
Stack different colored paper for a layered effect

www.paperdinosaurs.com
facebook.com/paperdinosaurs

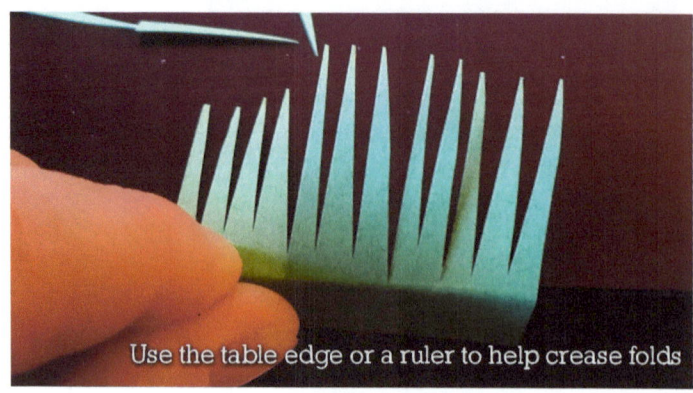
Use the table edge or a ruler to help crease folds

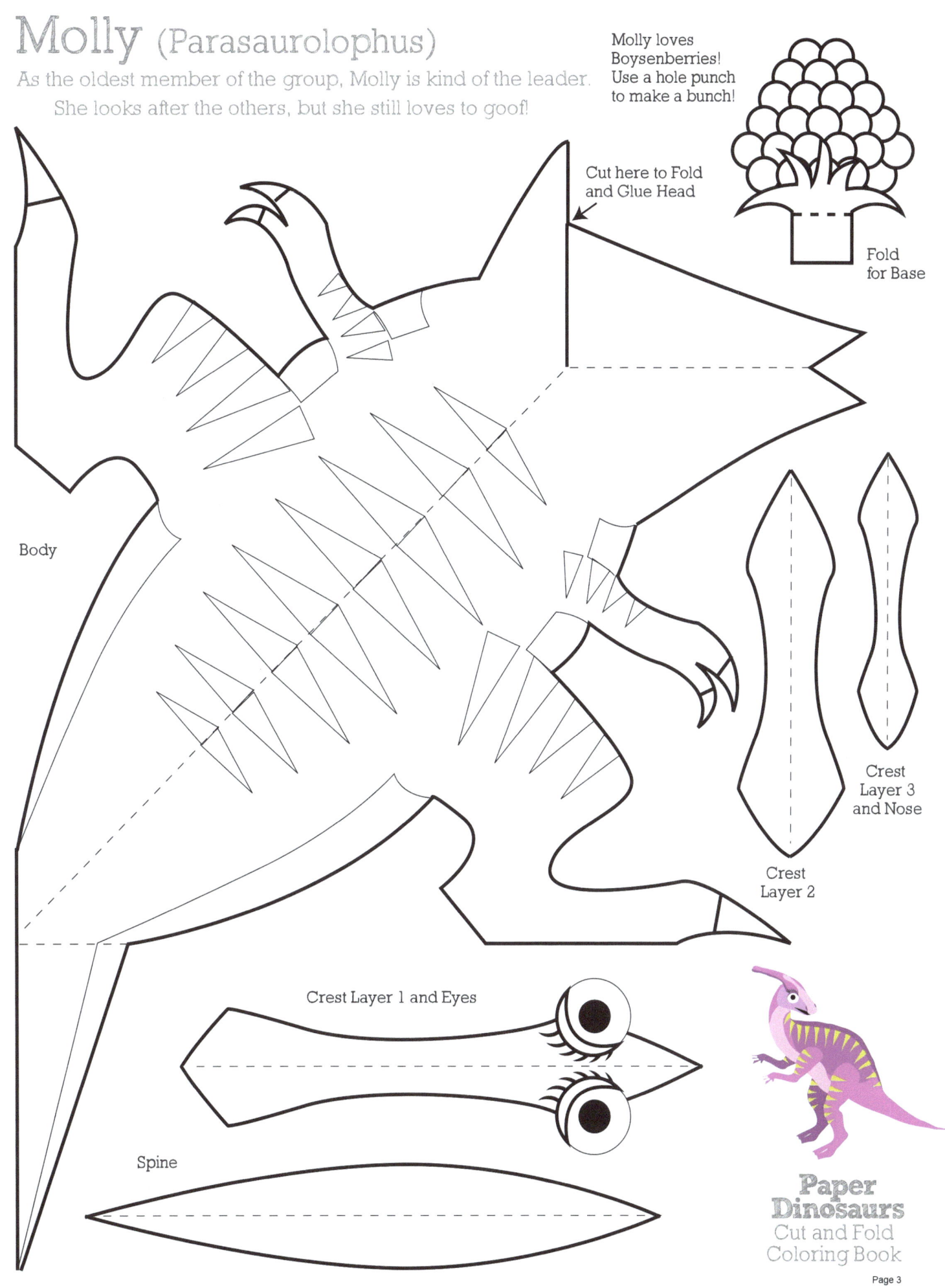

Molly B&W Backing

Each page of this book is meant to be torn out and cut up,
so this will be the backing color of your paper parts!

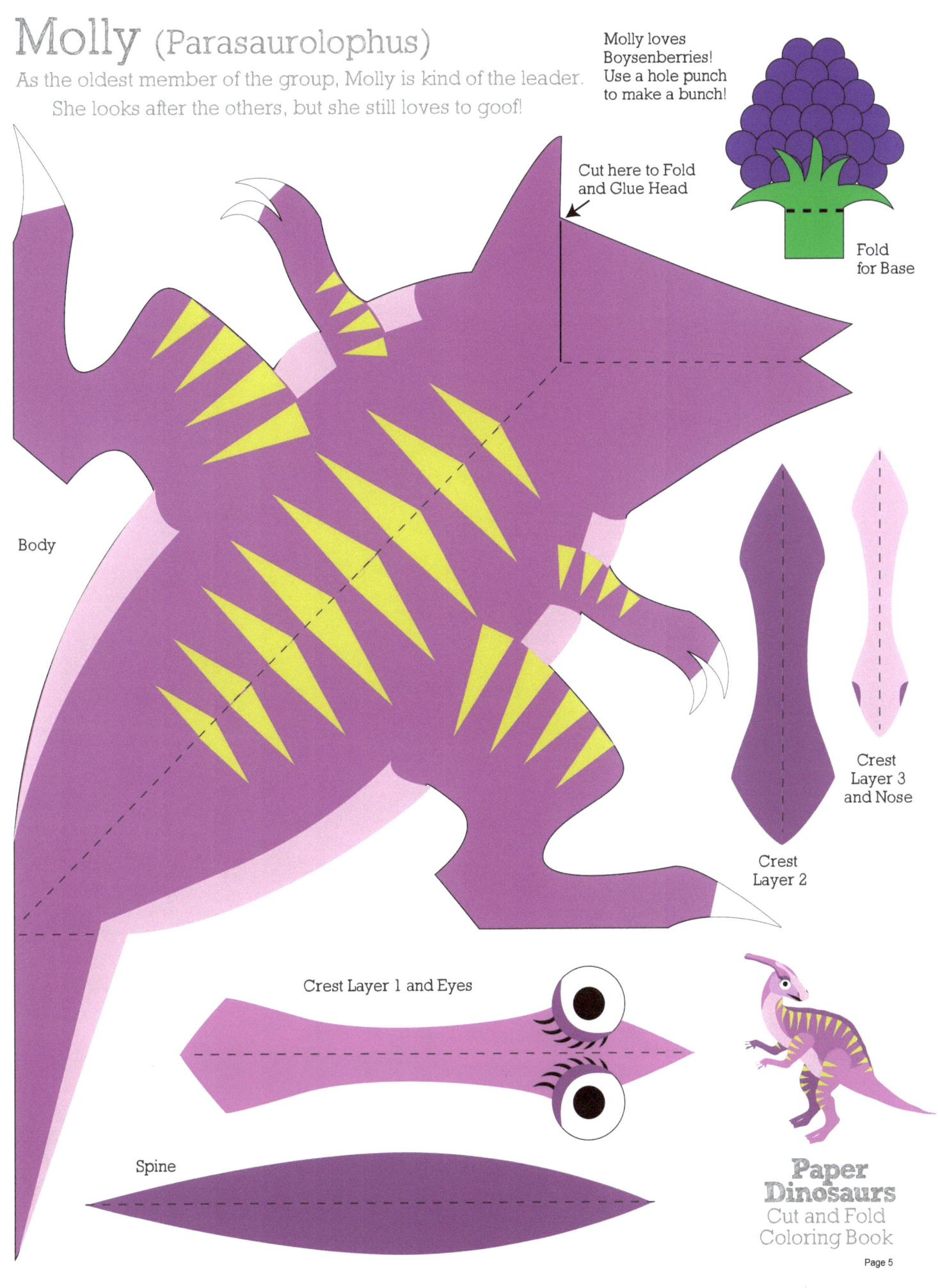

Molly Color Backing
Each page of this book is meant to be torn out and cut up, so this will be the backing color of your paper parts!

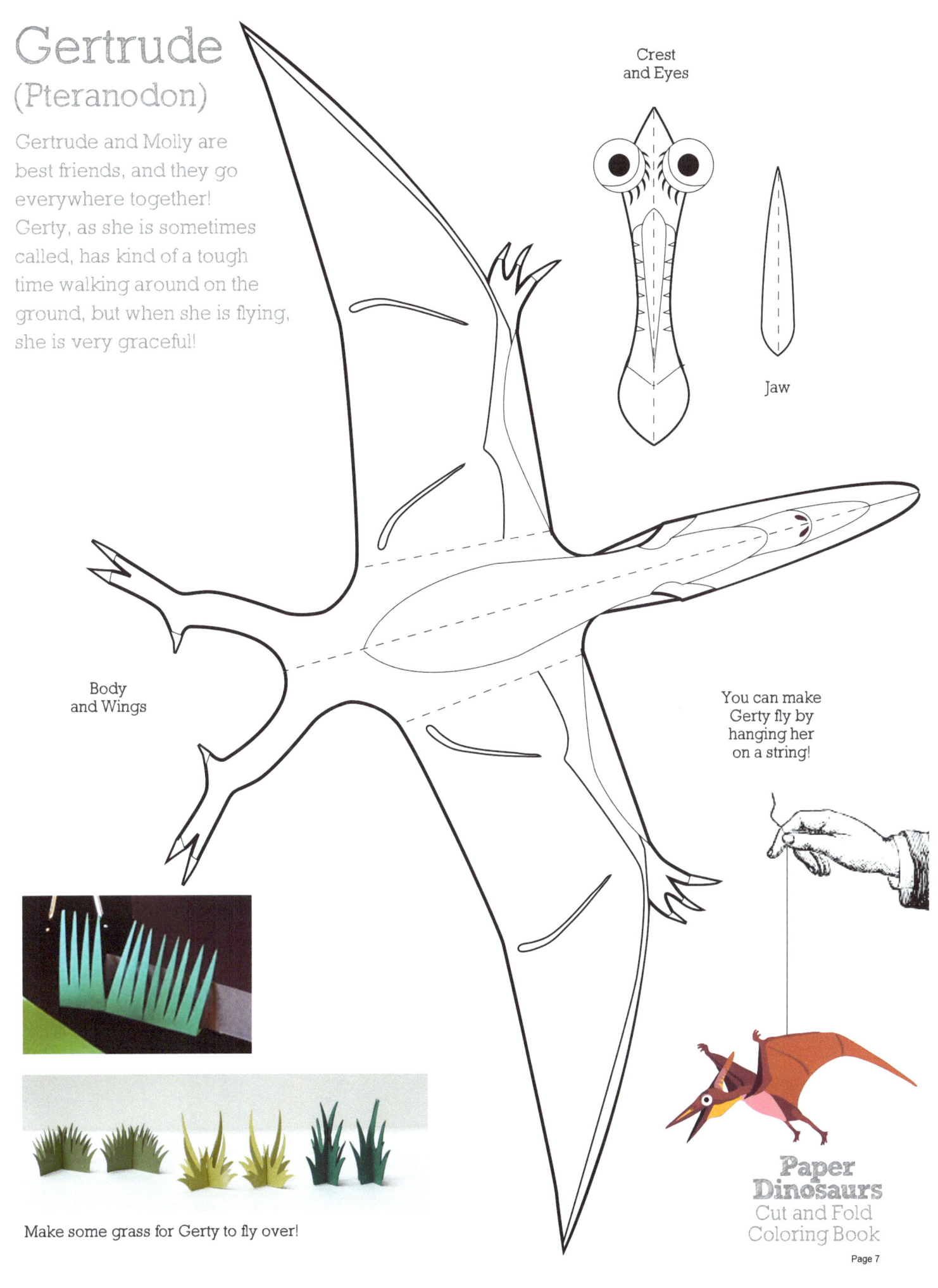

Gertrude
B&W Backing

Each page of this book is meant to be torn out and cut up, so this will be the backing color of your paper parts!

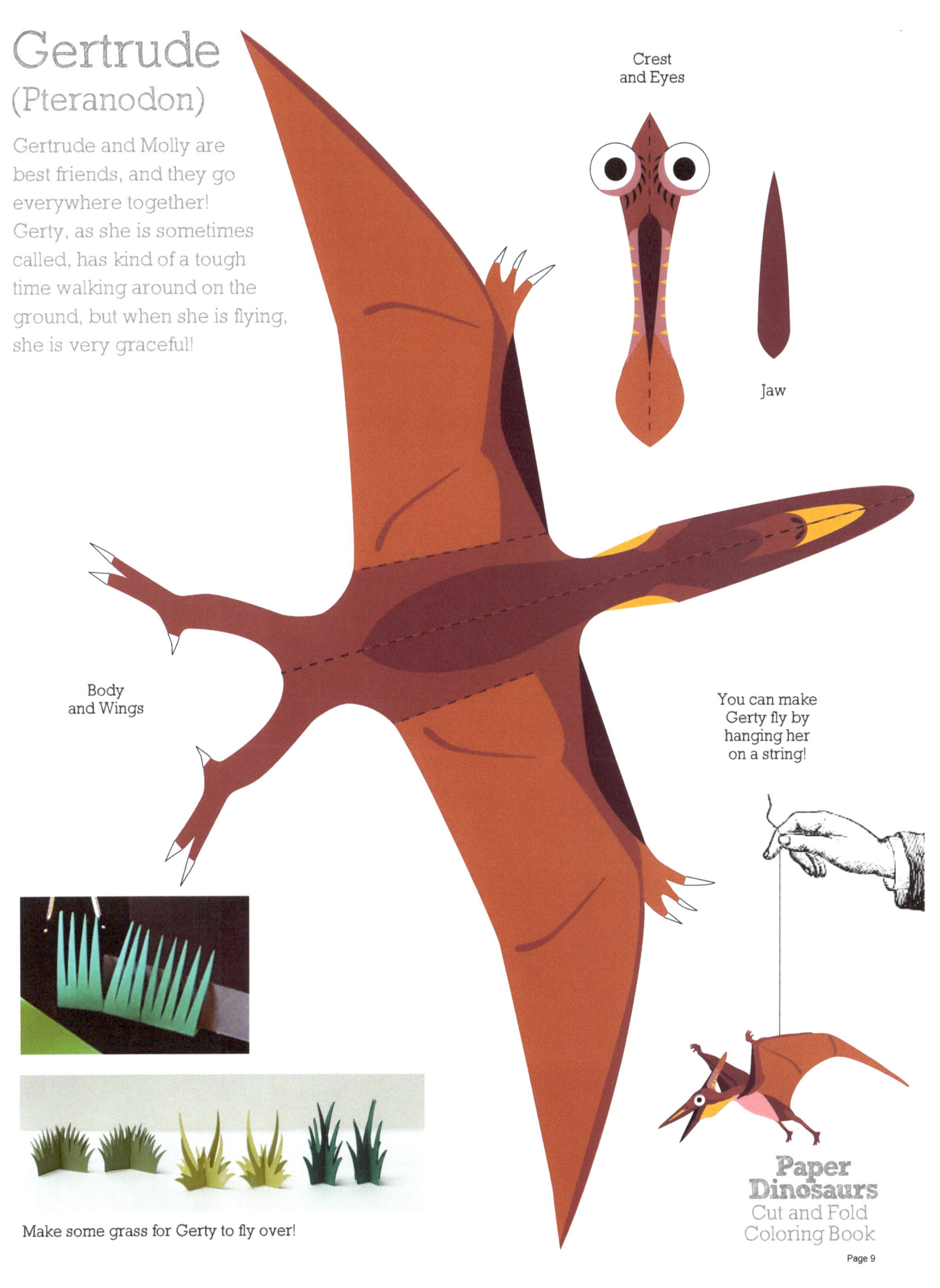

Gertrude
Color Backing

Each page of this book is meant to be torn out and cut up, so this will be the backing color of your paper parts!

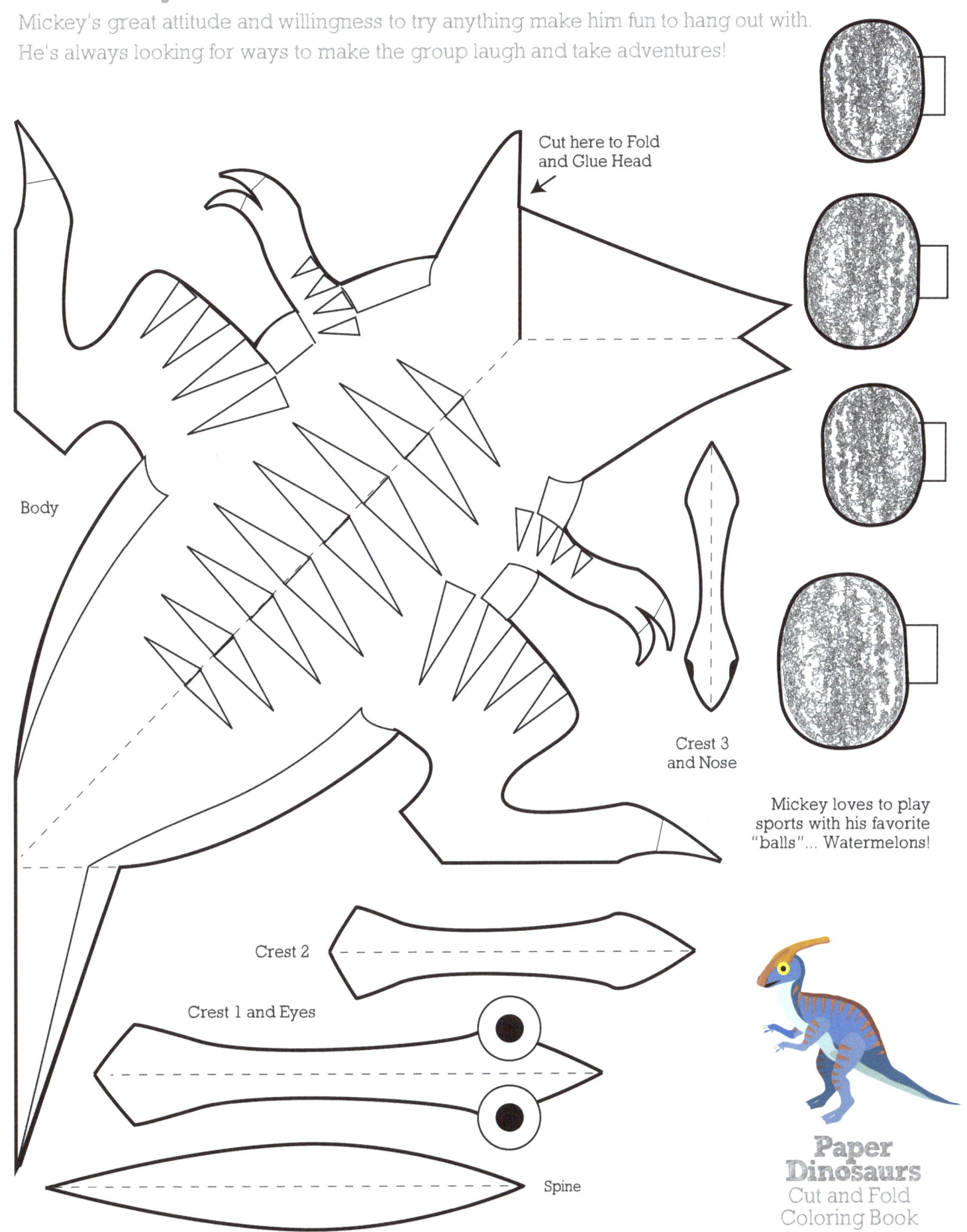

Mickey B&W Backing

Each page of this book is meant to be torn out and cut up, so this will be the backing color of your paper parts!

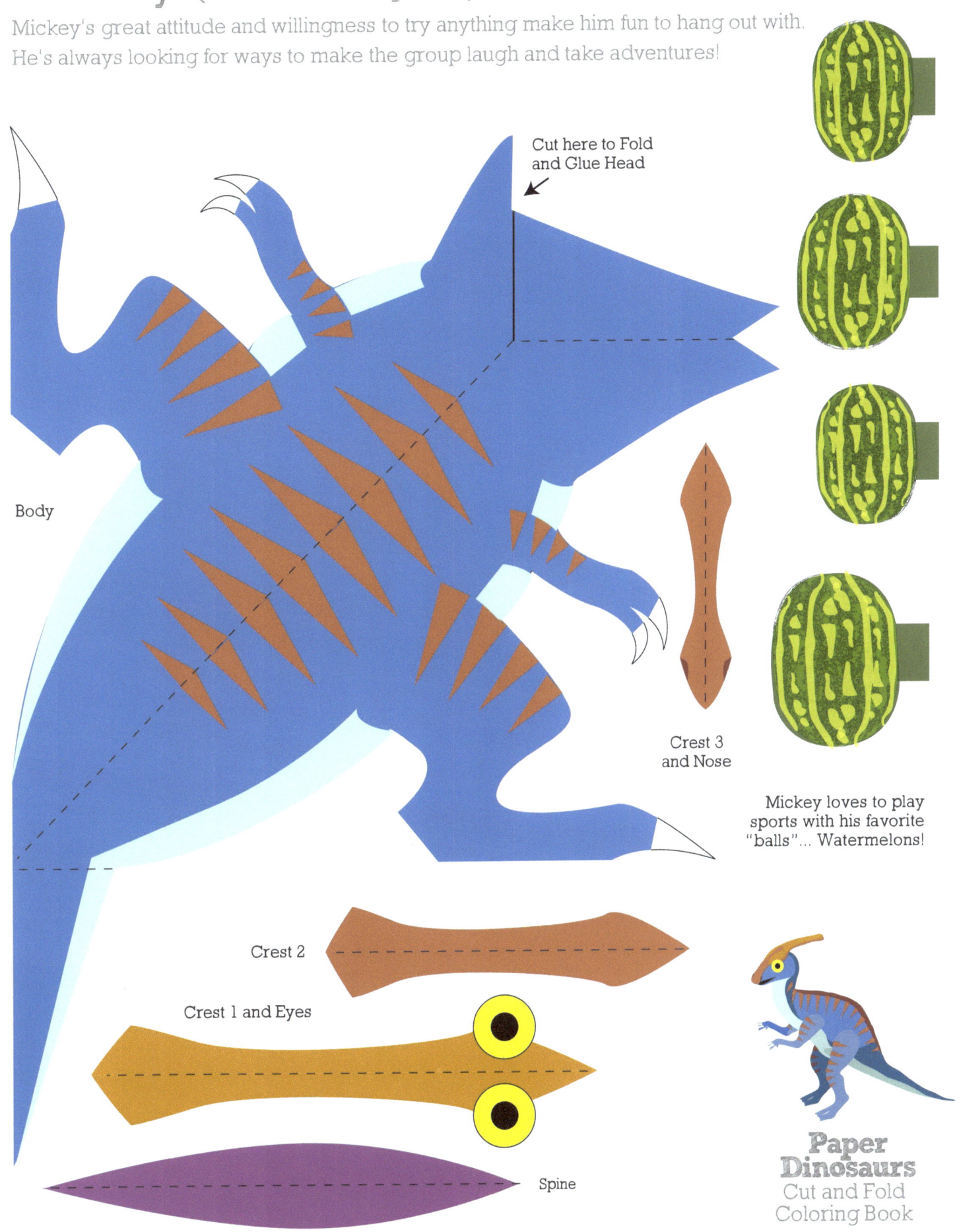

Mickey Color Backing

Each page of this book is meant to be torn out and cut up, so this will be the backing color of your paper parts!

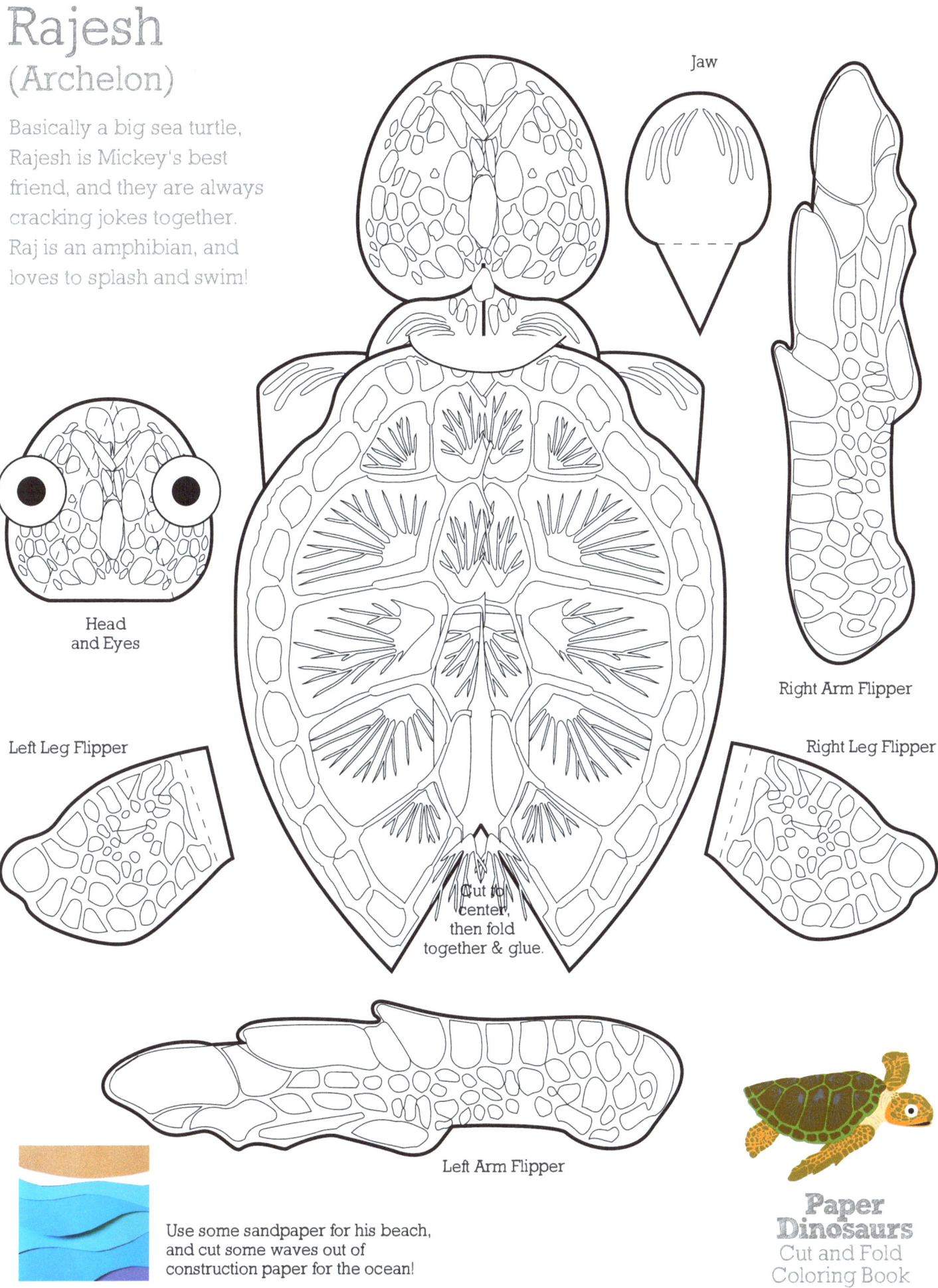

Rajesh
B&W Backing

Each page of this book is meant to be torn out and cut up, so this will be the backing color of your paper parts!

Rajesh
(Archelon)

Basically a big sea turtle, Rajesh is Mickey's best friend, and they are always cracking jokes together. Raj is an amphibian, and loves to splash and swim!

Jaw

Head and Eyes

Right Arm Flipper

Left Leg Flipper

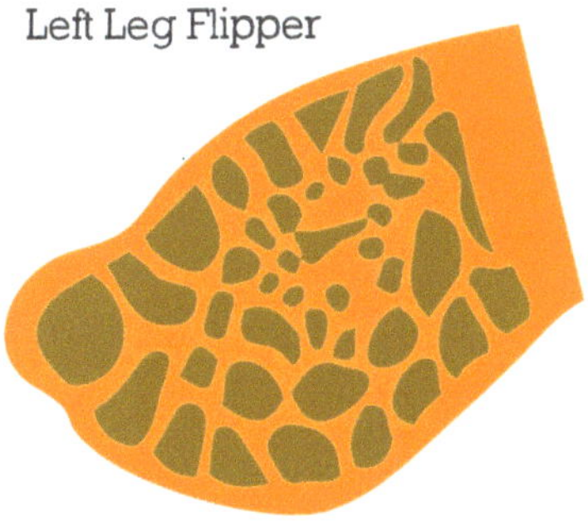

Right Leg Flipper

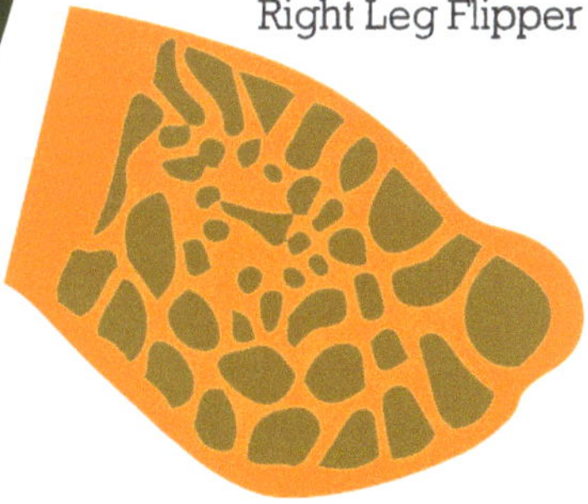

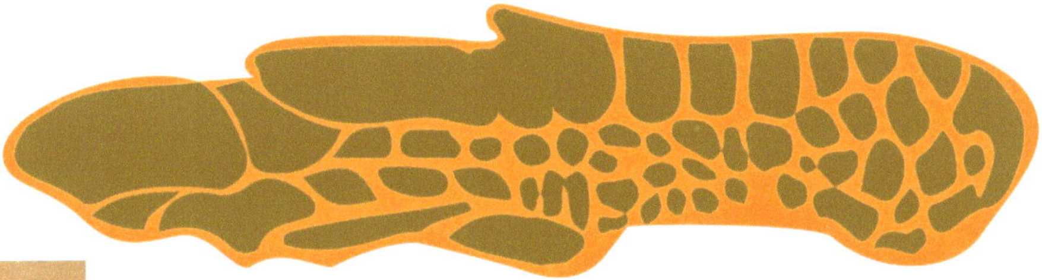

Cut to center, then fold together & glue.

Left Arm Flipper

Use some sandpaper for his beach, and cut some waves out of construction paper for the ocean!

Paper Dinosaurs
Cut and Fold Coloring Book

Page 17

Rajesh
Color Backing

Each page of this book is meant to be torn out and cut up, so this will be the backing color of your paper parts!

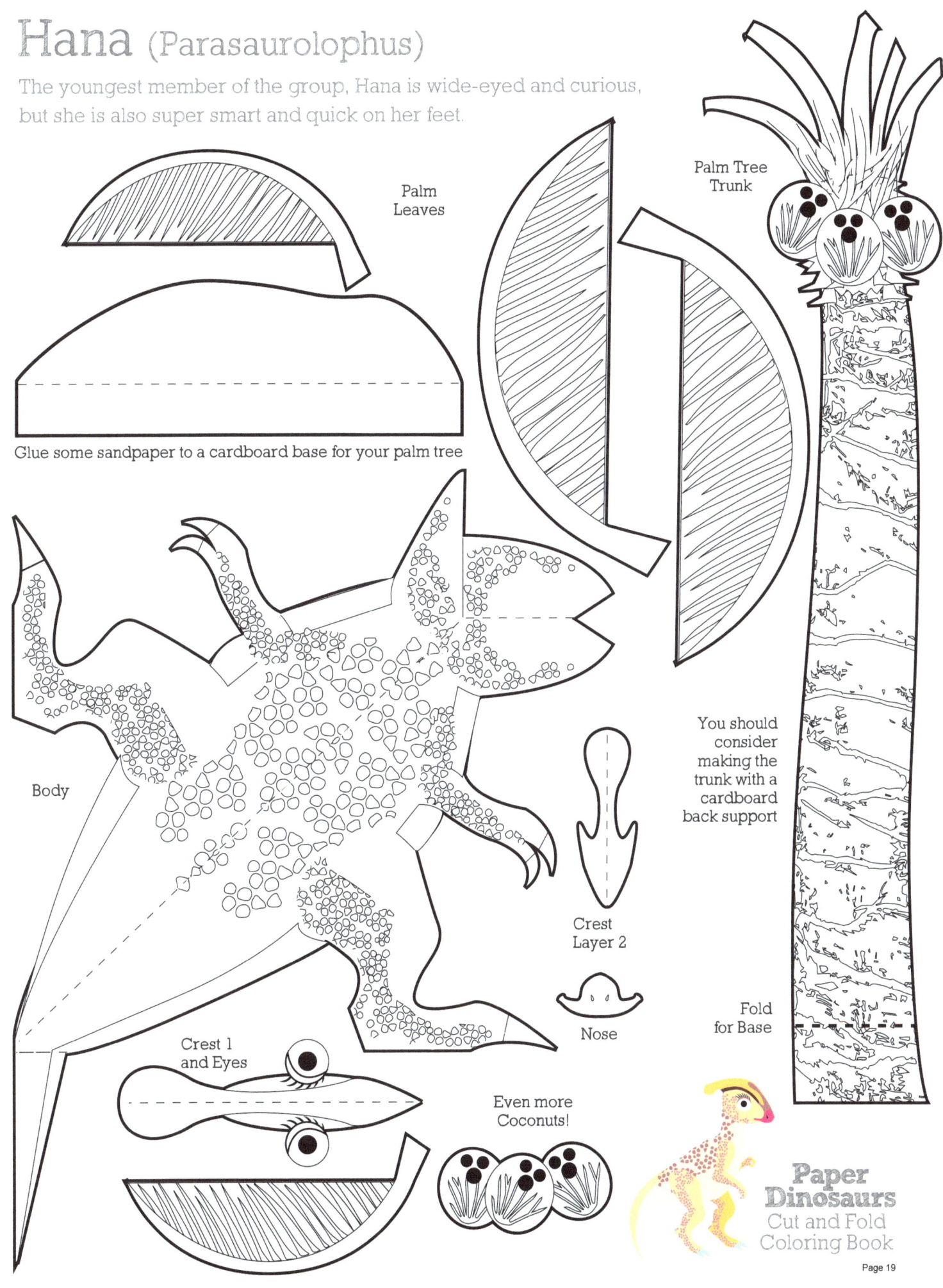

Hana B&W Backing

Each page of this book is meant to be torn out and cut up, so this will be the backing color of your paper parts!

Hana (Parasaurolophus)

The youngest member of the group, Hana is wide-eyed and curious, but she is also super smart and quick on her feet.

Palm Leaves

Palm Tree Trunk

Glue some sandpaper to a cardboard base for your palm tree

Body

You should consider making the trunk with a cardboard back support

Crest Layer 2

Nose

Fold for Base

Crest 1 and Eyes

Even more Coconuts!

Paper Dinosaurs
Cut and Fold Coloring Book

Hana Color Backing

Each page of this book is meant to be torn out and cut up, so this will be the backing color of your paper parts!

All about Paper Dinosaurs!

Welcome to Paper Pangea... Arts & Crafts and Fun & Games

Throughout this book, you have read a bit about Molly and Mickey and little Hana, the youngest member of the Parasaurolophus kids. Along with Mom and Dad, they live at the edge of the forest, where there are lots of fruits and veggies to eat! The forest is right on the outskirts of the beach, very close to the ocean, surrounded by cliffs on the distant shoreline.

You also read about Molly and Mickey's best friends, Gertrude the flying Pteranodon and Rajesh the amphibious Archelon. There are many different species of dinosaurs who live together in this part of Paper Pangea, and it's always a blast hanging out with the other dino kids!

So, what do Paper Dinosaurs do all day? Well, they do pretty much what all kids do... Play and learn! All the dino kids love to explore their prehistoric world. Some like to play sports, and some like to play music. They are always on the lookout for adventure, and, of course, new fruit to try! Add to that a lot of singing and dancing and silliness, and you pretty much have it :-)

www.paperdinosaurs.com
facebook.com/paperdinosaurs

Paper Dinosaurs
Cut and Fold Coloring Book

Paper Dinosaurs Paper Evolution!

I wrote the original story in 1996, when my twin boys were five. We went to the library to get some books on their favorite subject... Dinosaurs. They found a book on folding paper cats, but they really didn't want to build paper cats. They wanted to build Paper Dinosaurs! When we got home, we worked through the first designs of the characters and, using techniques from the paper cat book, we assembled our first Paper Dinosaurs. Plus, we learned a lot about the art of paper sculpting.

That night, I knocked out the first draft of the story of Molly and Mickey, and the rest of their family and friends, and the world of Paper Pangea. Over the years, as Justin and I developed the look of what was then going to be a cartoon series, we asked many of our art and animation friends to do their take on my early designs. We explored many different styles, and some of these were great, but not exactly right for what Justin and I had in mind for Paper Dinosaurs.

That is, until I met Diana Beltran Herrera, and saw the wonderful paper sculptures she was creating. Diana, originally from Columbia, has been making unique birds and flowers out of paper for years, and her style and technique were exactly what we needed! Of course, she totally loved the concept, and immediately nailed the designs and paper sculpts. After what seemed like an entire epoch of evolution, the look of Paper Dinosaurs was finally complete!

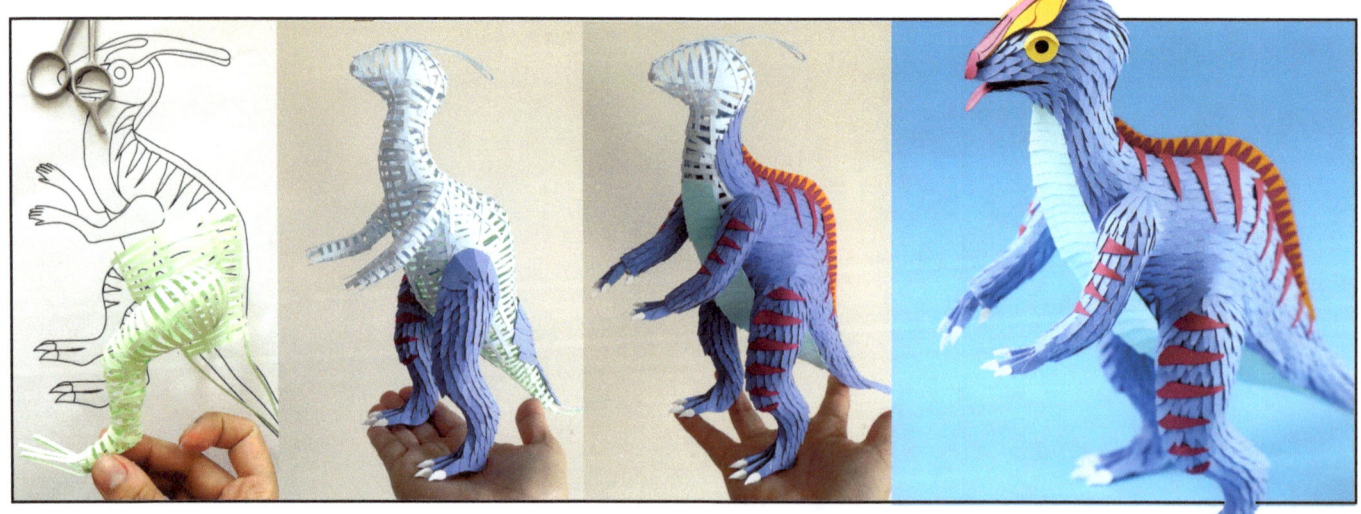

Here are some of her work in progress shots, as she built Mickey from the ground up! Diana's paper sculpts are much more detailed than those you'll find in this book, but with practice, you can build one like this, too. Mickey alone has over 250 hand crafted pieces!

In making this book, the biggest challenge was taking her designs, and simplifying them so that almost anybody could make one, or two, or more... In an afternoon! So, on behalf of all the paper paleontologists who have helped bring Paper Dinosaurs to life, we hope you enjoy them.

Thanks, and have some fun!

www.ingramcontent.com/pod-product-compliance
Lightning Source LLC
LaVergne TN
LVHW072103070426
835508LV00002B/247